Berries

Berries

4 Queen Street
Bath BA1 1HE, UK

Copyright © Parragon Books Ltd 2006

ISBN: 978-1-4454-0703-6

Printed in China

Internal design by Fiona Roberts
Produced by the Bridgewater Book Company Ltd
Photography by David Jordan
Home economy by Jacqueline Bellefontaine

Notes for the Reader
This book uses imperial, metric, and US cup measurements. Follow the same units of
measurement throughout; do not mix imperial and metric. All spoon measurements are
level: teaspoons are assumed to be 5 ml, and tablespoons are assumed to be 15 ml. Unless
otherwise stated, milk is assumed to be whole, eggs and individual vegetables such as
potatoes are medium, and pepper is freshly ground black pepper.

The times given are an approximate guide only. Preparation times differ according to the
techniques used by different people and the cooking times may also vary from those given
as a result of the type of oven used. Optional ingredients, variations or serving suggestions
have not been included in the calculations.

Recipes using raw or very lightly cooked eggs should be avoided by infants, the elderly,
pregnant women, convalescents, and anyone with a chronic condition. Pregnant and
breastfeeding women are advised to avoid eating peanuts and peanut products. Sufferers
from nut allergies should be aware that some of the ready-prepared ingredients used in the
recipes in this book may contain nuts. Always check the packaging before use.

Berries contain such a wide variety of nutrients that they have gained the status of "superfood." All red berries, for example, are rich in vitamin C, while blueberries are good for detoxing the body and maintaining body functions such as balance and coordination, circulation, and eyesight. Blackberries are high in fiber, folic acid, and vitamin C, and black currants have valuable antibacterial qualities.

The most common berries are strawberries, raspberries, and blackberries, as well as the ever-popular blueberry. Cranberries are delicious in cranberry sauce, pies, and desserts, while green gooseberries are excellent for pies and crumbles, and make a sharp, piquant sauce for oily fish and rich foods. Juniper berries, famous for flavoring gin, lend their pungent qualities to savory dishes, while tayberries, mulberries, loganberries, boysenberries, and huckleberries are becoming more easily available.

Although not strictly "berries," red currants and black currants are included in this book, since they are used in similar ways to true berries.

To enjoy berries at their best, use them fresh and when in season. Most berries are acceptable frozen when cooked in a recipe, apart from strawberries, which do not freeze well.

We all know how delicious berries are eaten fresh with cream or ice cream, or baked in pies and used in other fruit-based desserts, but here is the perfect opportunity to widen your perspective on berries. You will see in this collection of innovative recipes how effortlessly they add a whole new dimension to a wide variety of savory dishes to give an exciting taste sensation. And as an extra bonus, they contribute natural, vibrant color.

Start by dispelling your preconceptions with the delicious Strawberry Soup, which acts as a wonderful palate sharpener and is a much lighter alternative first course to a traditional soup. Berries are also great in salads, as you will soon discover, and instantly enhance them with their sun-ripened flavor—ideal for enjoying alfresco on a hot day. A tangy, piquant berry sauce or

THE MAIN EVENT

relish can transform simple broiled or pan-fried meat and poultry, and is a smart way to add to your five-a-day fruit and vegetable target. The sharpness of berries also has the ability to cut through the fattiness of some foods, such as duck, to improve their flavor and aid digestion.

All these recipes demonstrate how berries can be used to make tastier, healthier meals, and give an imaginative, contemporary twist to classic dishes.

SERVES 6

2 lb/900 g fresh strawberries

generous ¾ cup cranberry juice

generous ¾ cup dry white wine
    or apple juice

¾ cup sour cream

fresh mint sprigs, to garnish

Strawberry Soup

If you prefer, you can process the uncooked strawberries in a blender or food processor instead of cooking them, which gives a sharper flavor.

• Pick over the strawberries and hull. Reserve 1¾ cups. Put the remainder of the fruit in a large pan with the cranberry juice, and cook over medium heat until the fruit is softened.

• Let cool slightly, then transfer the fruit and juice to a blender or food processor and process until smooth.

• Add the wine, process briefly to combine, then pour into a pitcher. Cover with plastic wrap and chill in the refrigerator.

• Meanwhile, slice the reserved strawberries. Pour the soup into 6 bowls and float the sliced strawberries on top. Top with a spoonful of sour cream and garnish with mint sprigs. Serve immediately.

SERVES 6

1 lb/450 g salmon fillets, skinned

1 lb/450 g potatoes, peeled, boiled,
and mashed

2 tbsp chopped fresh parsley

grated rind of 1 lemon

2 tbsp heavy cream

1 tbsp all-purpose flour

1 egg, beaten

2 cups whole-wheat bread crumbs,
made from one-day old bread

4 tbsp vegetable oil,
for shallow-frying

salt and pepper

fresh salad, to serve

GOOSEBERRY SAUCE

8 oz/225 g fresh gooseberries

2 tbsp butter, softened

1–2 tbsp sugar, to taste

pinch of ground ginger (optional)

Salmon Fishcakes with Gooseberry Sauce

Try smoked trout or smoked mackerel instead of the salmon fillets—smoked fish does not need to be precooked.

• Put the fish in a large pan and just cover with water. Bring to a boil over medium heat, then reduce the heat and simmer gently, covered, for 5 minutes, or until cooked.

• Remove from the heat. Using a slotted spoon, lift the fish out onto a plate. When cool enough to handle, flake the fish roughly into bite-size pieces, ensuring that there are no stray bones.

• Mix the mashed potatoes with the fish, parsley, lemon rind, and cream. Season well with salt and pepper and shape into 6 round cakes.

• Put the flour, beaten egg, and bread crumbs into 3 separate shallow bowls. Dust the fishcakes with flour, then dip into the beaten egg and coat thoroughly in the bread crumbs. Transfer to a baking sheet and cover with plastic wrap, then chill in the refrigerator for at least 30 minutes.

• Meanwhile, make the sauce. Trim the gooseberries and put in a pan with a little cold water. Cook over low heat until the fruit is softened to a pulp. Remove from the heat and beat well with a wooden spoon until smooth, or transfer to a blender or food processor and process until smooth. Beat in the butter, and sugar to taste (gooseberries vary in their acidity). Add the ginger, if using, and transfer to a small serving bowl.

• Heat the oil in a skillet over medium heat. Pan-fry the fishcakes for 5 minutes on each side, turning them carefully with a spatula. Remove from the skillet and drain on paper towels.

• Serve the fishcakes with the sauce, accompanied by a fresh salad.

SERVES 6
12 oz/350 g couscous
2½ cups boiling chicken stock
    or vegetable stock
12 oz/350 g fresh raspberries
small bunch of fresh basil
8 oz/225 g feta cheese, cubed
    or crumbled

2 zucchini, thinly sliced
4 scallions, trimmed and
    diagonally sliced
⅓ cup pine nuts, toasted
grated rind of 1 lemon

DRESSING
1 tbsp white wine vinegar
1 tbsp balsamic vinegar
4 tbsp extra virgin olive oil
juice of 1 lemon
salt and pepper

Raspberry and Feta Salad with Couscous

Instead of couscous, you could use cracked wheat for a crunchier salad.

• Put the couscous in a large, heatproof bowl and pour over the stock. Stir well, then cover and let soak until all the stock has been absorbed.

• Pick over the raspberries, discarding any that are overripe. Shred the basil leaves.

• Transfer the couscous to a large serving bowl and stir well to break up any lumps. Add the cheese, vegetables, raspberries, and pine nuts. Stir in the basil and lemon rind and gently toss all the ingredients together.

• Put all the dressing ingredients in a screw-top jar, with salt and pepper to taste, then screw on the lid and shake until well blended. Pour over the salad and serve.

SERVES 4

1 smoked chicken, weighing
   3 lb/1.3 kg

scant 1 cup dried cranberries

2 tbsp apple juice or water

7 oz/200 g sugar snap peas

2 ripe avocados

juice of ½ lemon

4 lettuce hearts

1 bunch of watercress, trimmed

55 g/2 oz arugula

½ cup walnuts, chopped, to garnish
   (optional)

DRESSING

2 tbsp olive oil

1 tbsp walnut oil

2 tbsp lemon juice

1 tbsp chopped fresh mixed herbs,
   such as parsley and lemon thyme

salt and pepper

Smoked Chicken and Cranberry Salad

Dried cherries or other dried fruit can be used instead of cranberries.

• Carve the chicken carefully, slicing the white meat. Divide the legs into thighs and drumsticks and trim the wings. Cover with plastic wrap and refrigerate.

• Put the cranberries in a bowl. Stir in the apple juice, then cover with plastic wrap and let soak for 30 minutes.

• Meanwhile, blanch the sugar snap peas, then refresh under cold running water and drain.

• Peel, pit and slice the avocados, and toss in the lemon juice to prevent browning.

• Separate the lettuce hearts and arrange on a large serving platter with the avocados, sugar snap peas, watercress, arugula, and the chicken.

• Put all the dressing ingredients, with salt and pepper to taste, in a screw-top jar, then screw on the lid and shake until well blended.

• Drain the cranberries and mix them with the dressing, then pour over the salad.

• Serve immediately, scattered with walnuts, if using.

SERVES 4

4 skinless, boneless chicken breasts
    or 8 thighs
4 tbsp dry white wine or hard cider
2 tbsp chopped fresh rosemary
¼ tsp freshly grated nutmeg
pepper
fresh rosemary sprigs, to garnish
crisp green salad, to serve

BRAMBLE SAUCE

7 oz/200 g blackberries,
    plus extra to garnish
1 tbsp cider vinegar
2 tbsp red currant jelly

Skewered Chicken with Bramble Sauce

This autumnal recipe can be made with freshly picked wild blackberries from the hedgerow if you are lucky enough to have a good local supply. If you have to use canned fruit, omit the red currant jelly.

• Using a sharp knife, cut the chicken into 1-inch/2.5-cm pieces and put in a bowl. Sprinkle over the wine and chopped rosemary and season well with pepper. Cover and let marinate in the refrigerator for at least an hour.
• Preheat the broiler to medium-high. Drain the chicken, reserving the marinade, and thread the meat onto 8 metal skewers, or wooden skewers presoaked in cold water for 30 minutes.
• Cook the chicken under the broiler, turning the skewers occasionally, for 8–10 minutes, or until golden brown, tender, and cooked through.
• Meanwhile, to make the sauce, put the reserved marinade in a pan with the blackberries and cook over low heat until the fruit is softened. Using the back of a wooden spoon, press the mixture through a nylon strainer into a bowl to form a purée.
• Return the blackberry purée to the pan, then add the vinegar and red currant jelly and bring to the boil. Boil, uncovered, until the sauce is reduced by about one-third.
• Spoon a little sauce onto each plate and put two chicken skewers on top. Sprinkle with the nutmeg and serve hot, garnished with rosemary sprigs and blackberries, accompanied by a green salad.

SERVES 4

1 lb/450 g boneless duck breasts

2 tbsp raspberry vinegar

2 tbsp brandy

1 tbsp clear honey

1 tsp corn oil, for brushing

salt and pepper

2 kiwifruit, peeled and thinly sliced,
   to serve

BERRY SAUCE

8 oz/225 g raspberries,
   thawed if frozen

1¼ cups rosé wine

2 tsp cornstarch, blended with
   4 tsp cold water

Duck with Berry Sauce

If you can't find raspberry vinegar, you can instead use red wine vinegar.

• Skin the duck breasts and discard any excess fat. Using a sharp knife, score the flesh of each duck breast in diagonal lines and pound it with a covered rolling pin or meat mallet until it is ¾ inch/2 cm thick.

• Put the duck breasts in a shallow, non-metallic dish. Mix the vinegar, brandy, and honey together in a small bowl and spoon it over the duck. Cover with plastic wrap and let marinate in the refrigerator for about an hour.

• Preheat the broiler to medium. Drain the duck, reserving the marinade, and put on the broiler rack. Season to taste with salt and pepper and brush with oil. Cook under the broiler for 10 minutes, then turn over; season to taste with salt and pepper and brush with oil again. Cook for an additional 8–10 minutes or until the meat is tender and cooked through.

• Meanwhile, to make the sauce, reserve about ⅓ cup of the raspberries and put the remainder in a pan. Add the reserved marinade and the wine. Bring to a boil, then reduce the heat and simmer for 5 minutes, or until slightly reduced. Using the back of a spoon, press the mixture through a nylon strainer into a bowl to form a purée.

• Return the purée to the pan and stir in the cornstarch paste. Cook, stirring constantly, until thickened. Add the reserved raspberries and season to taste with salt and pepper.

• Thinly slice the duck breast. Serve with slices of kiwifruit on warmed serving plates with the sauce spooned over.

SERVES 4

4 thick legs of lamb chops, about
  7–9 oz/200–250 g each and
  1 inch/2.5 cm thick

MARINADE

2 garlic cloves, sliced

4 fresh rosemary sprigs,
  plus extra to garnish

2 tbsp olive oil

½ cup red wine

salt and pepper

RED CURRANT SAUCE

8 oz/225 g fresh red currants or
  cranberries, plus extra to garnish

scant ¼ cup superfine sugar

1 tbsp balsamic vinegar

¾ cup red wine

pinch of ground cinnamon

grated rind of 1 orange

TO SERVE

new potatoes tossed in
  chopped fresh mint

green vegetables

Broiled Lamb Chops with Red Currant Sauce

The Red Currant Sauce can be made in advance and reheated when needed. You can also grill the lamb chops.

• Arrange the lamb chops in a single layer in a shallow, non-metallic dish. Scatter over the garlic and rosemary. Pour over the oil and wine and season well with salt and pepper. Cover with plastic wrap and let marinate in the refrigerator for at least 2 hours, or preferably overnight.

• Meanwhile, make the sauce. Strip the red currants from their stems using the prongs of a fork and put in a small pan with the sugar, vinegar, and wine over low heat. Bring slowly to a simmer, then add the cinnamon and orange rind. Cook gently until the red currants are softened and the sauce is a good consistency. Beat with a wooden spoon to make a coarse purée. Using the back of a wooden spoon, press the mixture through a nylon strainer into a bowl to remove the seeds.

• When you are ready to cook the chops, preheat the broiler to high. Remove the chops from the marinade, discarding any slices of garlic and rosemary sprigs. Cook the chops under the broiler for 2–3 minutes on one side, depending on how you like your lamb cooked. Turn the chops over and cook until done to taste.

• Serve immediately with the sauce, new potatoes, and green vegetables, garnished with rosemary sprigs and red currants.

SERVES 4

4 veal scallops, about 6 oz/175 g each

2 tbsp butter

1 tbsp corn or vegetable oil

2 shallots, finely chopped

1 cooking apple, peeled, cored, and
    finely chopped

2 tbsp raw brown sugar

½ tsp ground ginger

2 tbsp balsamic vinegar

5½ oz/150 g fresh blackberries

salt and pepper

crisp green salad, to serve

Veal Scallops with Blackberry and Apple Relish

You could use veal or pork chops in this recipe instead of scallops—they would need to be cooked for longer because they are thicker.

• Preheat the oven to 300°F/150°C. Put the scallops between 2 sheets of plastic wrap and beat with a rolling pin or a meat mallet until thin.

• Heat the butter in a skillet over high heat and cook the scallops for 2–3 minutes on each side until lightly browned. You may need to do this in 2 batches if the scallops are large. Remove from the skillet and season well with salt and pepper, then keep warm in the preheated oven.

• Heat the oil in the skillet and cook the shallots until softened. Add the apple, sugar, ginger, and vinegar to the skillet, then stir well and cook for 3–4 minutes, or until the apple is softened. Add the blackberries and cook for an additional 2–3 minutes, or until the relish is well reduced and all the fruit is softened. Season to taste with salt and pepper.

• Put the scallops onto warmed serving plates and serve with a crisp green salad and the relish alongside.

SERVES 4
½ fennel bulb
1 tbsp juniper berries
2 tbsp olive oil
finely grated rind and juice of
   1 orange
4 pork chops, about
   5½ oz/150 g each

TO SERVE
crisp green salad
fresh bread

Pork with Fennel and Juniper Berries

Juniper berries are often added to Italian meat dishes for a delicate citrus flavor. They can be bought dried from health-food stores and supermarkets.

- Trim and finely chop the fennel bulb, discarding the green parts.
- Crush the juniper berries in a mortar with a pestle. Mix with the fennel, oil, and orange rind in a bowl.
- Using a sharp knife, score the flesh of each pork chop in diagonal lines. Put the chops in a roasting pan or ovenproof dish. Spoon the fennel and juniper berry mixture over the top. Pour over the orange juice, then cover with plastic wrap and let marinate in the refrigerator for about 2 hours.
- Preheat the broiler to medium. Place the pork chops in the roasting pan under the broiler and cook, turning occasionally, for 10–15 minutes, depending on the thickness of the meat, or until the meat is tender and cooked through.
- Transfer the chops to serving plates and serve with a crisp green salad and plenty of fresh bread to mop up the cooking juices.

SERVES 4

8 good-quality sausages

1 tbsp corn or vegetable oil

MARMALADE

3 tbsp olive oil

14 oz/400 g red onions,
  halved and finely sliced

2/3 cup red wine

2 tbsp balsamic vinegar

1/4 cup dark muscovado sugar

8 oz/225 g fresh cranberries

TO SERVE

mashed potato

green vegetables

Sausages with Cranberry and Red Onion Marmalade

The marmalade can be stored in an airtight container in the refrigerator for up to 1 week and can be served warm or cold with salads and cold cuts. It is also perfect for serving with roast turkey for Thanksgiving.

• Preheat the oven to 400°F/200°C. Put the sausages in a small roasting pan and pour over the corn oil. Roll the sausages in the oil until well coated.

• Roast the sausages in the preheated oven for 25–30 minutes. Alternatively, cook the sausages in a skillet over low heat, turning occasionally, until well browned and sticky.

• Meanwhile, to make the marmalade heat the olive oil in a wide pan and cook the onions over medium heat, stirring frequently to prevent them sticking to the pan, for 10–15 minutes, or until very soft and browned. Add the wine, vinegar, and sugar and stir until the sugar has dissolved. Cook for an additional 10 minutes, or until the liquid is reduced and the onions are sticky.

• Add the cranberries and stir well. Cook for 4–5 minutes, or until the cranberries have burst and the mixture is the consistency of chutney. Remove the marmalade from the heat and serve with the sausages, mashed potato, and green vegetables.

In this chapter, we see how berries can be used to create delicious, healthy breakfasts and snacks, as well as lighter bites to fit today's busy lifestyles. But let's not forget that they can also be at the heart of some truly indulgent dishes, too.

Berries make the perfect, nutritious way to start the day, either in a classic cereal or in a modern-style smoothie. Quick and easy to prepare, the drinks also make a refreshing snack at any time of the day and are a healthier alternative to processed snacks such as cookies and crisps. But when it's the weekend and you feel in need of something a little more luxurious, choose from Blueberry Pancakes with warm maple syrup and Spiced French Toast with Seasonal Berries for a late breakfast or brunch.

A LIGHT MOMENT

In the afternoon, why not try a fresh, healthy take on that perennial favorite of biscuits, preserve, and cream—Banana Bread with Strawberry Compote and Mascarpone, flavored with warm, sweet spices. In fact, this is substantial enough to be served as a brunch or to eat as a between-meal snack. But if it's the taste of days gone by that you crave, you can't beat real homemade preserve, just like grandma used to make. Even if you have time to make only one batch of four or five jars, it will be a real treat for you and your family.

SERVES 2

generous 1 cup jumbo oats

generous ¾ cup apple juice

1 red apple, cored

1 tbsp lemon juice

scant ¼ cup chopped toasted
hazelnuts

½ tsp ground cinnamon

scant ½ cup plain yogurt

2 tbsp runny honey (optional)

2½ oz/70 g fresh bilberries or
blueberries

Bilberry Bircher Granola

If bilberries or blueberries are unavailable, substitute any other fresh berries. Add a sliced banana for a more substantial snack.

• Put the oats and apple juice in a bowl, then cover with plastic wrap and let soak in the refrigerator for an hour, or overnight.

• Grate or chop the apple and mix with the lemon juice to prevent browning.

• Add the apple, hazelnuts, and cinnamon to the oat mixture and mix well.

• Spoon the mixture into serving bowls and top with the yogurt. Drizzle over the honey, if using. Spoon the bilberries over the granola and serve.

MAKES 10–12

1 cup all-purpose flour

2 tbsp superfine sugar

2 tbsp baking powder

½ tsp salt

scant 1 cup buttermilk

3 tbsp unsalted butter, melted

1 large egg

5 oz/140 g fresh blueberries, plus
    extra to serve

sunflower-seed or corn oil, for oiling

TO SERVE

butter

warm maple syrup

Blueberry Pancakes

When it's summer in Maine, the state's blueberries seemingly feature at every meal, starting with breakfast, when they flavour muffins and pancakes. For a complete New England breakfast, serve these with Vermont maple syrup.

• Preheat the oven to 275°F/140°C. Sift the flour, sugar, baking powder, and salt together into a large bowl and make a well in the center.

• Beat the buttermilk, butter, and egg together in a separate small bowl, then pour the mixture into the well in the dry ingredients. Beat the dry ingredients into the liquid, gradually drawing them in from the side, until a smooth batter is formed. Gently stir in the blueberries.

• Heat a large skillet over medium-high heat until a splash of water dances on the surface. Using a pastry brush or crumpled piece of paper towel, oil the base of the skillet.

• Drop about 4 tablespoons of batter separately into the skillet and spread each out into a 4-inch/10-cm circle. Continue adding as many pancakes as will fit in your skillet. Cook until small bubbles appear on the surface, then flip over with a spatula and cook the pancakes on the other side for an additional 1–2 minutes, or until the bases are golden brown.

• Transfer the pancakes to a plate and keep warm in the preheated oven while you cook the remaining batter, lightly oiling the skillet as before. Make a stack of the pancakes with parchment paper in between each pancake.

• Serve with a knob of butter on top of each pancake, extra blueberries on the side and warm maple syrup for pouring over.

SERVES 4

4 eggs, plus 1 extra egg white

¼ tsp ground cinnamon

¼ tsp allspice

4 slices thick white bread

1 tbsp unsalted butter, melted

fresh mint sprigs, to decorate

BERRIES

scant ½ cup superfine sugar

¼ cup freshly squeezed orange juice

10½ oz/300 g mixed fresh seasonal

berries, such as strawberries,

raspberries, and blueberries,

picked over and hulled

Spiced French Toast with Seasonal Berries

This oven-baked method of making French Toast uses much less fat than the shallow-fried version and makes it easy to produce larger quantities.

• Preheat the oven to 425°F/220°C. Put the eggs and egg white in a large, shallow bowl or dish and whisk together with a fork. Add the cinnamon and allspice and whisk until combined.

• To prepare the berries, put the sugar and orange juice in a pan and bring to a boil over low heat, stirring until the sugar has dissolved. Add the berries, then remove from the heat and let cool for 10 minutes.

• Meanwhile, soak the bread slices in the egg mixture for about 1 minute on each side. Brush a large baking sheet with the melted butter and place the bread slices on the sheet. Bake in the preheated oven for 5–7 minutes, or until lightly browned. Turn the slices over and bake for an additional 2–3 minutes. Serve the berries spooned over the toast and decorated with mint sprigs.

MAKES 5 X 1-LB/450-G JARS
3 lb 8 oz/1.6 kg fresh strawberries
3 tbsp lemon juice
3 lb/1.3 kg granulated or preserving
   sugar

Strawberry Preserve

Strawberries have little pectin in them to help set the preserve, so it is important to add the lemon juice.

• Preheat the oven to 350°F/180°C. Sterilize five 1-lb/450-g preserve jars with screw-top lids.
• Pick over the strawberries, discarding any that are overripe, and hull. Put the fruit in a large pan with the lemon juice and heat over low heat until some of the fruit juices begin to run. Continue to simmer gently for 10–15 minutes, or until softened.
• Add the sugar and stir until it has dissolved. Increase the heat and boil rapidly for 2–3 minutes, or until setting point is reached. Test the mixture with a sugar thermometer— it should read 221°F/105°C for a good setting point. Alternatively, drop a teaspoonful of preserve onto a cold saucer and place it in the refrigerator to cool it, and then push it with your finger. If it forms a wrinkled skin, it is ready. If not, boil for an additional minute and repeat.
• Remove the pan from the heat and let cool for 15–20 minutes, to prevent the fruit rising in the jar. Skim the preserve if necessary.
• Meanwhile, warm the jars in the preheated oven. Remove and fill carefully with the preserve, using a ladle and a preserve funnel. Top with waxed disks, waxed-side down, and screw on the lids tightly. Wipe the jars clean and let cool. Label and date to avoid confusion later.
• Store in a cool, dry place. Once opened, it is advisable to keep the jar in the refrigerator.

MAKES 4 X 1 LB/450 G JARS

3 lb/1.3 kg granulated or preserving
  sugar

2 lb 4 oz/1 kg fresh raspberries

Quick Raspberry Preserve

If the raspberries have a lot of seeds, you can strain some of the preserve before filling the jars to reduce the amount.

• Preheat the oven to 325°F/160°C. Sterilize four 1-lb/450-g preserve jars with screw-top lids.

• Put the sugar in a large, heatproof bowl and warm in the preheated oven.

• Meanwhile, pick over the raspberries, discarding any that are overripe. Put the fruit in a large pan and heat over low heat until some of the fruit juices begin to run. Simmer gently for 2–3 minutes, or until softened.

• Add the warmed sugar and stir until it has dissolved. Increase the oven temperature to 350°F/180°C.

• Increase the heat and boil the preserve rapidly for 2–3 minutes. Remove from the heat and let cool for 2 minutes. Skim if necessary.

• Meanwhile, warm the jars in the oven. Remove and fill carefully with the preserve, using a ladle and a preserve funnel. Top with waxed disks, waxed-side down, and screw on the lids tightly. Wipe the jars clean and let cool. Label and date to avoid confusion later.

• Store in a cool, dry place. Once opened, it is advisable to keep the jar in the refrigerator. This preserve does not have a very firm set, but it does have a delicious flavor.

SERVES 8
1⅛ sticks butter, softened,
    plus extra for greasing
½ cup superfine sugar
¼ cup soft brown sugar
3 eggs
1 tsp vanilla extract
3 large, ripe bananas

1⅔ cups self-rising flour
1 tsp freshly grated nutmeg
1 tsp ground cinnamon
confectioners' sugar, sifted, for
    dusting (optional)
mascarpone cheese or plain yogurt,
    to serve

STRAWBERRY COMPOTE
scant ½ cup soft brown sugar
juice of 2 oranges
grated rind of 1 orange
1 cinnamon stick
14 oz/400 g fresh strawberries,
    hulled and thickly sliced

Banana Bread with Strawberry Compote and Mascarpone

The bread can be stored in the freezer for up to three months. Thaw overnight in the refrigerator before serving. It can also be iced for a delicious treat.

• Preheat the oven to 350°F/180°C. Grease a 9 x 4¼-inch/23 x 11-cm loaf pan and line the base with nonstick parchment paper.

• Put the butter and sugars in a bowl and beat together until light and fluffy. Mix in the eggs, one at a time, then mix in the vanilla extract. Peel the bananas and mash roughly with the back of a fork. Stir gently into the butter mixture, then add the flour, nutmeg, and cinnamon, stirring until just combined.

• Pour the mixture into the prepared pan and bake in the preheated oven for 1¼ hours, or until a skewer inserted into the center comes out clean. Let stand in the pan for 5 minutes before turning out onto a wire rack to cool.

• To make the compote, put the sugar, orange juice and rind, and cinnamon stick in a pan and bring to a boil. Add the strawberries and return to a boil. Remove from the heat, then pour into a clean heatproof bowl and let cool. Remove the cinnamon stick. Serve slices of the banana bread with a dollop of mascarpone cheese or yogurt and spoon over the warm or cold compote. Dust with sifted confectioners' sugar if desired.

SERVES 2

4 tbsp orange juice

1 tbsp lime juice

scant ½ cup sparkling water

4 ice cubes

12 oz/350 g frozen summer berries,
    such as blueberries, raspberries,
    blackberries, and strawberries

whole fresh strawberries,
    raspberries, black currants,
    and blackberries on toothpicks,
    to decorate

Summer and Citrus Fruit Punch

To give this punch a fragrant twist, substitute dry ginger ale for the sparkling water. For an alcoholic version, replace the sparkling water with sparkling white wine.

• Pour the orange juice, lime juice, and sparkling water into a blender or food processor and process gently until well-combined.

• Put the ice cubes between 2 clean cloths and crush with a rolling pin. Add to the blender with the frozen berries and process until a slushy consistency has been reached.

• Pour the mixture into glasses, then decorate with whole strawberries, raspberries, black currants, and blackberries on toothpicks and serve.

SERVES 2

¾ cup milk

8 oz/225 g canned peach slices
(drained weight)

2 fresh apricots, chopped

14 oz/400 g fresh strawberries

2 fresh bananas, sliced and frozen

Strawberry and Peach Smoothie

You can easily vary this recipe to make different flavored smoothies. Use raspberries or blueberries in place of the strawberries, or a small peeled, pitted mango instead of the apricots. Or try replacing the bananas with a couple of scoops of vanilla or even chocolate ice cream.

• Pour the milk into a blender or food processor. Add the peach slices and gently process until combined. Add the apricots and gently process again until combined.

• Pick over the strawberries and hull, reserving 1 to decorate. Add the strawberries and frozen banana slices and process until smooth. Pour the mixture into glasses. Slice the reserved strawberry and use to decorate the glasses. Serve immediately.

We are going back to traditional cooking in this chapter, and the art of making cakes and other baked treats and desserts. Home baking is not just rewarding in creating memorable food for family and friends, but is in itself highly therapeutic. Mixing a cake by hand in the calm and warmth of the kitchen can provide a soothing retreat from the hurly-burly of our busy lives. And the results of your labors will always be welcomed by the recipients—children in particular. They might even help and get to lick the mixing bowl!

Here we have some long-established desserts, such as crumble and cobbler, elevated out of the everyday with the addition of succulent berries and currants. Other firm family favorites include muffins, shortcake, and cheesecake, made sumptuous with

SWEET TREATS

blueberries, strawberries, and gooseberries. But you don't have to wait for dessert to enjoy fruit-filled delights. Those old faithful lunch-box or picnic companions, brownies and oat-style cookies, are enriched here with luscious loganberries and chewy dried cranberries and blueberries, and will provide an energy-boosting snack when you're on the move, or a delicious afternoon treat.

The whole range of berries can be used in these recipes—ring the changes by substituting other berries or currants, or use what's readily available. Whatever you choose, the results will be more than satisfying.

MAKES 10–12

1⅔ cups all-purpose flour

1 tsp baking powder

pinch of salt

½ cup raw brown sugar,
   plus 1 tbsp for sprinkling

1 egg, beaten

scant 1 cup milk

4 tbsp unsalted butter, melted

4½ oz/125 g small fresh blueberries

Blueberry Muffins

These muffins are delicious served warm. They are best eaten on the day of baking, because they do not store well.

• Preheat the oven to 350°F/180°C. Line a 12-hole muffin pan with muffin paper cases.

• Sift the flour, baking powder, and salt into a large bowl and stir in the sugar.

• Add the beaten egg, milk, and melted butter to the dry ingredients and stir in lightly until just combined—do not overmix. Carefully fold in the blueberries.

• Spoon the mixture into the paper cases, taking care not to overfill, and sprinkle with the remaining sugar.

• Bake in the preheated oven for 25–30 minutes, or until golden brown and firm. Transfer to a wire rack to cool a little.

MAKES 9–12

1½ sticks unsalted butter, plus extra
    for greasing
6 squares bittersweet chocolate,
    broken into pieces
scant 1¼ cups golden superfine
    sugar

pinch of salt
3 large eggs, beaten
generous ¾ cup all-purpose flour
6 oz/175 g fresh loganberries

Loganberry and Chocolate Brownies

These brownies can
be served with ice cream
and some loganberry sauce
for a delicious dessert.

• Preheat the oven to 350°F/180°C. Grease and line an 8-inch/20-cm square cake pan with a sheet of nonstick parchment paper.

• Put the butter and chocolate in a large, heatproof bowl, then set the bowl over a pan of barely simmering water and heat until melted. Stir until smooth, then remove from the heat and let cool slightly.

• Stir the sugar and salt into the chocolate mixture, then gradually beat in the eggs.

• Sift the flour into the mixture and beat until smooth. Carefully stir in the loganberries.

• Scrape the mixture into the prepared pan and bake in the preheated oven for 25–30 minutes, or until the top is pale brown but the middle is dense and gooey.

• Remove from the oven and let cool in the pan slightly before cutting into squares (cut to the size you prefer).

• Let cool completely before removing from the pan. Peel off the lining paper.

SERVES 8
scant 1¼ cups self-rising flour
⅞ stick unsalted butter, diced and
    chilled, plus extra for greasing
generous ⅓ cup superfine sugar
1 egg yolk

1 tbsp rose water
2½ cups whipping cream,
    lightly whipped
8 oz/225 g fresh strawberries, hulled
    and cut into fourths, plus a few
    whole strawberries, to decorate

TO DECORATE
fresh strawberry leaf or mint leaves
confectioners' sugar

Strawberry Shortcake

The shortcake can be
made a few days in
advance and stored in
an airtight container
until required.

• Preheat the oven to 375°F/190°C. Lightly grease 2 baking sheets.
• To make the shortcakes, sift the flour into a bowl. Rub in the butter with your fingers until the mixture resembles bread crumbs. Stir in the sugar, then add the egg yolk and rose water and mix to form a soft dough.
• Divide the dough in half. Roll out each piece into a 7½-inch/19-cm circle and transfer each one to a prepared baking sheet. Crimp the edges of the dough.
• Bake in the preheated oven for 15 minutes, or until lightly golden. Transfer the shortcakes to a wire rack to cool.
• Mix the cream with the strawberry quarters and spoon on top of one of the shortcakes. Top with the other shortcake circle. Decorate with whole strawberries and a strawberry leaf or mint leaves, and dust with a little confectioners' sugar.

MAKES 18

2 sticks unsalted butter, plus extra
  for greasing
1 cup light muscovado sugar
scant ⅓ cup corn syrup

1 lb/450 g porridge oats
2 tsp ground cinnamon
4 oz/115 g dried berries
  (cranberries and blueberries
  are often sold together)

Fruity Oat-Style Cookies

These cookies can be stored in an airtight container for up to 3–4 days. Honey can be used in place of the corn syrup for a slightly less sweet version.

• Preheat the oven to 350°F/180°C. Line an 8 x 12-inch/20 x 30-cm deep baking pan with a sheet of nonstick parchment paper.

• Put the butter, sugar, and syrup in a pan and heat over low heat until melted.

• Add the porridge oats and cinnamon and stir well. Add the dried berries and stir to distribute them evenly throughout the oats.

• Pour the mixture into the prepared baking pan, then press down well and bake in the center of the preheated oven for 30–35 minutes, or until golden-brown but still moist and slightly soft when pressed.

• Remove from the oven and let cool for 5 minutes. Cut into 18 pieces and let cool completely before removing from the pan.

MAKES 12

PASTRY

1⅓ cups all-purpose flour,
    plus extra for dusting

¾ cup confectioners' sugar

½ cup ground almonds

1 stick unsalted butter,
    diced and chilled

1 egg yolk

1 tbsp milk

FILLING

1½ cups unsalted cream cheese

confectioners' sugar, to taste,
    plus extra for dusting

12 oz/350 g fresh summer berries
    and currants, such as blueberries,
    raspberries, small strawberries,
    red currants, and white currants,
    picked over and prepared

Summer Fruit Tartlets

If you wash the summer fruit just before using it, be sure to drain well on paper towels, otherwise the liquid will make the pastry shells soggy.

• To make the pastry, sift the flour and sugar into a bowl, then stir in the almonds. Rub in the butter with your fingertips until the mixture resembles bread crumbs. Add the egg yolk and milk and mix to form a dough. Turn out onto a lightly floured counter and knead briefly. Wrap and chill in the refrigerator for 30 minutes.

• Preheat the oven to 400°F/200°C. Roll out the pastry and use it to line 12 deep tartlet or individual brioche pans. Prick the pastry bottoms with a fork. Press a piece of foil into each tartlet, covering the edges, and bake in the preheated oven for 10–15 minutes, or until light golden-brown. Remove the foil and bake for an additional 2–3 minutes. Transfer the pastry shells to a wire rack to cool.

• To make the filling, mix the cream cheese and sugar together in a bowl. Put a spoonful of filling in each pastry shell and arrange the fruit on top. Dust with sifted confectioners' sugar and serve immediately.

SERVES 4

9 oz/250 g fresh blueberries

9 oz/250 g fresh raspberries

9 oz/250 g fresh blackberries

½ cup superfine sugar

2 tbsp confectioners' sugar,
   to decorate

light cream, to serve

PASTRY

1⅓ cups all-purpose flour,
   plus extra for dusting

¼ cup ground hazelnuts

⅞ stick unsalted butter, diced and
   chilled, plus extra for greasing

finely grated rind of 1 lemon

1 egg yolk, beaten

4 tbsp milk

Forest Fruit Pie

You could use other kinds of berries in this pie, such as loganberries or bilberries. Ground hazelnuts and lemon rind are added to the pastry for extra flavor, but you could substitute ground pistachios and lime rind for an alternative taste.

• Pick over the berries and put in a pan with 3 tablespoons of the superfine sugar and cook over medium heat, stirring frequently, for 5 minutes. Remove from the heat.

• To make the pastry, sift the flour into a bowl, then stir in the hazelnuts. Rub in the butter with your fingertips until the mixture resembles bread crumbs, then sift in the remaining superfine sugar. Add the lemon rind, egg yolk, and 3 tablespoons of the milk and mix to form a dough. Turn out onto a lightly floured counter and knead briefly. Wrap with plastic wrap and chill in the refrigerator for 30 minutes.

• Preheat the oven to 375°F/190°C. Grease an 8-inch/20-cm pie dish with butter. Roll out two-thirds of the pastry to a thickness of ¼ inch/ 5 mm and use it to line the bottom and side of the dish. Spoon the berries into the pastry shell. Brush the rim with water, then roll out the remaining pastry and use it to cover the pie. Trim and crimp round the edge, then make 2 small slits in the top and decorate with 2 leaf shapes cut out from the dough trimmings. Brush all over with the remaining milk. Bake in the preheated oven for 40 minutes.

• Dust the pie with the confectioners' sugar and serve with light cream.

SERVES 6
PASTRY
2²/₃ cups all-purpose flour,
    plus extra for dusting
pinch of salt
1¼ sticks unsalted butter,
    diced and chilled
¼ cup superfine sugar
5 tsp semolina
1 egg white

FILLING
1 lb 10 oz/750 g fresh blackberries
6 tbsp golden superfine sugar
1 tbsp crème de cassis

CASSIS CREAM
1 cup heavy cream
1 tbsp crème de cassis

Bramble Tart with Cassis Cream

This tart can also be made with a mixture of berries and fruit—mix some raspberries, sliced strawberries, or slices of ripe plum or peach in with the blackberries. Use a non-alcoholic blackberry-flavored cordial in place of the cassis. This tart is also good served with ice cream.

• To make the pastry, sift the flour and salt into a large bowl and rub in the butter with your fingertips until the mixture resembles bread crumbs. Stir in the superfine sugar and add enough cold water to form a dough. Turn out onto a lightly floured counter and knead briefly. Wrap with plastic wrap and chill in the refrigerator for 30 minutes.
• Meanwhile, pick over the blackberries, then put in a bowl with 4 tablespoons of the golden superfine sugar and the cassis and stir to coat. Preheat the oven to 400°F/200°C.
• Roll out the pastry into a large circle, handling it carefully because it is quite a soft dough. Leave the edges ragged and place on a baking sheet. Sprinkle the pastry with the semolina, leaving a good 2¹/₂-inch/6-cm margin around the edge. Pile the fruit into the middle and brush the edges of the pastry with some of the egg white. Fold in the edge of the pastry to overlap and enclose the fruit, making sure to press the pastry together in order to close any gaps. Brush with the remaining egg white and sprinkle with the remaining sugar, then bake in the preheated oven for 25 minutes.
• Meanwhile, to make the Cassis Cream, whip the cream in a bowl until it begins to thicken, then stir in the cassis.
• Serve the tart hot, straight from the oven, with a good dollop of the Cassis Cream.

SERVES 6

2 lb/900 g fresh berries and currants,
    such as blackberries, blueberries,
    raspberries, red currants, and
    black currants
about ½ cup superfine sugar
2 tbsp cornstarch

COBBLER TOPPING

1⅓ cups all-purpose flour
2 tsp baking powder
pinch of salt
4 tbsp unsalted butter,
    diced and chilled

2 tbsp superfine sugar
¾ cup buttermilk
1 tbsp raw brown sugar
light or heavy cream, to serve

Fruit Cobbler

Instead of buttermilk,
you can use milk with
a good squeeze of
lime juice added.

• Preheat the oven to 400°F/200°C. Pick over the fruit, then mix with the superfine sugar and cornstarch and put in a 10-inch/25-cm shallow, ovenproof dish.

• To make the topping, sift the flour, baking powder, and salt into a large bowl. Rub in the butter until the mixture resembles bread crumbs, then stir in the superfine sugar. Pour in the buttermilk and mix to a soft dough.

• Drop spoonfuls of the dough on top of the fruit roughly, so that it doesn't completely cover the fruit. Sprinkle with the raw brown sugar and bake in the preheated oven for 25–30 minutes, or until the crust is golden and the fruit is tender.

• Remove from the oven and let stand for a few minutes before serving with cream.

SERVES 4

2 lb/900 g cooking apples

10½ oz/300 g blackberries,
    fresh or frozen

generous ¼ cup light
    muscovado sugar

1 tsp ground cinnamon

custard or pouring cream, to serve

CRUMBLE

generous ½ cup self-rising flour

¾ cup whole-wheat all-purpose flour

1 stick unsalted butter

generous ¼ cup raw brown sugar

Apple and Blackberry Crumble

When making a
crumble, keep rubbing
in the butter until the
crumbs are quite coarse.
This ensures that the
crumble will be crunchy.

• Preheat the oven to 400°F/200°C. Peel and core the apples, then cut into chunks. Put in a bowl with the blackberries, muscovado sugar, and cinnamon, and mix together, then transfer to an ovenproof baking dish.

• To make the crumble, sift the self-rising flour into a bowl and stir in the whole-wheat flour. Rub in the butter with your fingertips until the mixture resembles coarse bread crumbs. Stir in the raw brown sugar.

• Spread the crumble over the apples and bake in the preheated oven for 40–45 minutes, or until the apples are soft and the crumble is golden brown and crisp. Serve with custard or pouring cream.

SERVES 8–10

9 squares bittersweet chocolate,
   broken into pieces
2 sticks unsalted butter,
   plus extra for greasing
1 tbsp strong, dark coffee
5 eggs

½ cup golden superfine sugar
generous ½ cup all-purpose flour
1 tsp ground cinnamon
6 oz/175 g fresh raspberries,
   plus extra to serve
confectioners' sugar, for dusting
whipped cream, to serve

Raspberry Dessert Cake

If fresh raspberries are not available, you can use frozen raspberries. Since these will be softer than fresh fruit, take care to thaw them thoroughly and drain off any excess juice.

• Preheat the oven to 325°F/160°C. Grease a 9-inch/23-cm cake pan and line the base with nonstick parchment paper. Put the chocolate, butter, and coffee in a small, heatproof bowl, then set the bowl over a pan of barely simmering water and heat until melted. Remove from the heat and stir, then let cool slightly.

• Beat the eggs and superfine sugar together in a separate bowl until pale and thick. Gently fold the chocolate mixture into the egg and sugar mixture.

• Sift the flour and cinnamon into another bowl, then fold into the chocolate mixture. Pour into the prepared pan and sprinkle the raspberries evenly over the top.

• Bake in the preheated oven for about 35– 45 minutes, or until the cake is well risen and springy to the touch. Let cool in the pan for 15 minutes before turning out onto a large serving plate. Dust with confectioners' sugar before serving with fresh raspberries and whipped cream.

SERVES 8
BASE
4 tbsp unsalted butter
8 oz/225 g graham crackers, crushed
generous ⅓ cup chopped walnuts

FILLING
1 lb/450 g mascarpone cheese
2 eggs, beaten
½ cup superfine sugar
9 squares white chocolate,
    broken into pieces
9 oz/250 g gooseberries

TOPPING
6 oz/175 g mascarpone cheese
white and semisweet chocolate curls
16 whole strawberries

Gooseberry Cheesecake

You can make chocolate curls quickly and easily by running a swivel-bladed vegetable peeler down the side of a chunky bar of chocolate.

• Preheat the oven to 300°F/150°C. To make the base, melt the butter in a pan over low heat and stir in the crushed crackers and nuts. Spoon the mixture into a 9-inch/23-cm loose-bottom cake pan and press evenly over the base with the back of a spoon. Set aside.
• To make the filling, beat the cheese in a bowl until smooth, then beat in the eggs and 3 tablespoons of the sugar.
• Put the chocolate in the top of a double boiler over low heat or in a heatproof bowl set over a pan of barely simmering water and stir until melted and smooth. Remove from the heat and let cool slightly.
• Put the gooseberries and remaining sugar in a pan and heat over low heat, stirring, until the sugar has dissolved. Cook gently for 1–2 minutes, or until the gooseberries are softened but still whole. Let cool.
• Add the cooled chocolate and gooseberries to the filling. Spoon the mixture over the cracker base, then spread out evenly and smooth the surface. Bake in the preheated oven for 1 hour, or until the filling is just firm. Turn off the oven, but let the cheesecake stand in the oven until it is completely cold.
• Transfer the cheesecake to a serving plate and spread the mascarpone cheese on top. Decorate with chocolate curls and whole strawberries.

Desserts are where berries really come into their own. We all love the simple pleasure of eating freshly picked summer berries just as they come, but they can also be enjoyed in many different creative dishes that take very little time and effort to prepare. For instance, the addition of some whipped cream and a little sugar swirled into a berry purée makes a delectable, eye-catching fruit dessert, and what could be easier than dipping berries into melted semisweet chocolate, either to be eaten immediately fondue-style, or to be left for the chocolate to harden before serving as petits fours at the end of a meal? It's not just the taste of berries that is wonderful—a mixture of different chocolate-dipped berries, with their jewel-like colors and pleasing shapes and textures, makes a great centerpiece for a dinner party.

THE PERFECT FINALE

But sometimes something more extravagant is called for to provide a fitting finale to a special-occasion meal. A soufflé never fails to provide the wow factor, and the recipe here features an imaginative combination of cranberries and orange. Trifles are another success story, and here we have a delicious recipe of raspberries and strawberries laced with a berry liqueur.

As the season progresses, berries tend to become larger and softer, and this plump quality makes them ideal for cooking. The resulting purées make delicious ice-cold berry sherbets—wonderfully refreshing on a hot day or a balmy summer's evening.

SERVES 4–6
3 eggs, separated
2 envelopes granulated gelatin
3 tbsp orange juice
$2/3$ cup heavy cream, whipped until
soft and thick

$1/3$ cup finely chopped almonds,
toasted
orange zest, to decorate
$2/3$ cup light cream, to serve (optional)

CRANBERRY PURÉE
14 oz/400 g cranberries,
fresh or frozen
$2/3$ cup water
scant 1 cup superfine sugar
grated rind of 2 oranges

Cranberry and Orange Soufflé

To make a proper soufflé, use a 6-inch/15-cm soufflé dish and tie a double layer of parchment paper around the outside with string. The paper should stand up above the rim of the dish by $1\,1/4$ inches/3 cm. Brush the inside of the paper with oil. Once chilled, carefully remove the paper collar and gently press the nuts onto the side of the soufflé.

• First make the cranberry purée. Put the cranberries, water, and a generous $1/4$ cup of the sugar in a pan and cook over low heat for 2–3 minutes, or until the sugar has dissolved and the berries have formed a rich syrup. Let cool. Using the back of a wooden spoon, press through a nylon strainer into a bowl to form a purée. You should get about $1\,1/4$ cups. Stir in the orange rind.

• Whisk the egg yolks and remaining sugar with an electric mixer until thick and light.

• Put the gelatin in a heatproof cup with the orange juice and soak for 1–2 minutes, or until it is spongy. Put the cup in a small pan with enough water to come halfway up the sides and heat over low heat for 2–3 minutes, until the gelatin has dissolved and the mixture is clear. Let cool until it is the same temperature as the fruit purée, then stir into the fruit purée.

• Fold the fruit purée evenly into the egg mixture and then fold in the whipped cream.

• Whisk the egg whites in a grease-free bowl until stiff but not too dry and then fold gently into the mixture.

• Pour the mixture into a glass serving dish and smooth the top with a palette knife. Chill in the refrigerator for 3–4 hours, or until firm.

• Decorate with the nuts and orange zest and serve with a little cream poured over the top, if using.

MAKES 8–10
generous ⅔ cup all-purpose flour
scant ¼ cup unsweetened cocoa
pinch of salt
1 egg

2 tbsp superfine sugar
1½ cups milk
scant 2 tbsp unsalted butter
confectioners' sugar, for dusting
ice cream or pouring cream, to serve

BERRY COMPOTE
5½ oz/150 g fresh blackberries
5½ oz/150 g fresh blueberries
8 oz/225 g fresh raspberries
generous ¼ cup superfine sugar
juice of ½ lemon
½ tsp allspice (optional)

Chocolate Crêpes with Berry Compote

For a more indulgent dessert, serve with hot chocolate sauce made by melting 4 squares of bittersweet chocolate with ½ cup heavy cream.

• Preheat the oven to 275°F/140°C. Sift the flour, unsweetened cocoa, and salt together into a large bowl and make a well in the center.

• Beat the egg, sugar, and half the milk together in a separate bowl, then pour the mixture into the dry ingredients. Beat the dry ingredients into the liquid, gradually drawing them in from the side, until a batter is formed. Gradually beat in the remaining milk. Pour the batter into a pitcher.

• Heat a 7-inch/18-cm nonstick skillet over medium heat and add 1 teaspoon of the butter.

• When the butter has melted, pour in enough batter just to cover the bottom, then swirl it round the skillet while tilting it so that you have a thin, even layer. Cook for 30 seconds and then lift up the edge of the crêpe to check if it is cooked. Loosen the crêpe around the edge, then flip it over with a spatula or palette knife. Alternatively, toss the crêpe by flipping the skillet quickly with a flick of the wrist and catching it carefully. Cook on the other side until the bottom is golden brown.

• Transfer the crêpe to a warmed plate and keep warm in the preheated oven while you cook the remaining batter, adding the remaining butter to the skillet as necessary. Make a stack of the crêpes with parchment paper in between each crêpe.

• To make the compote, pick over the berries and put in a pan with the sugar, lemon juice, and allspice, if using. Cook over low heat until the sugar has dissolved and the berries are warmed through. Do not overcook.

• Put a crêpe on a warmed serving plate and spoon some of the compote onto the center. Either roll or fold the crêpe and dust with confectioners' sugar. Repeat with the remaining crêpes. Serve with ice cream or pouring cream.

SERVES 8

3 large eggs

generous ½ cup superfine sugar

scant 1 cup all-purpose flour

1 tbsp hot water

⅛ cup slivered almonds, toasted

1 tsp confectioners' sugar

FILLING

generous ¾ cup mascarpone

1 tsp almond extract

5½ oz/150 g small fresh blueberries

1 tbsp superfine sugar

Blueberry Roulade

To prevent the sponge from breaking when you roll it up with the filling in place, manipulate it with the parchment paper, not your fingers, and work slowly and carefully.

• Preheat the oven to 425°F/220°C. Line a 14 x 10-inch/35 x 25-cm jelly roll pan with nonstick parchment paper. Put the eggs in a large, heatproof bowl with the superfine sugar, then set over a pan of hot water and, using an electric whisk, whisk until pale and thick.

• Remove the bowl from the pan. Sift the flour, then fold into the egg mixture with the hot water. Pour the mixture into the prepared pan and bake in the preheated oven for 8–10 minutes, or until golden and set.

• Transfer the sponge to a sheet of nonstick parchment paper. Peel off the lining paper and roll up the sponge tightly with the parchment paper. Wrap in a clean dish towel and let cool.

• Meanwhile, to make the filling, mix the mascarpone and almond extract together in a bowl. Reserve a few blueberries for decoration, then put the remainder in a separate bowl and sprinkle with the superfine sugar. Cover the mascarpone mixture and the fruit with plastic wrap. Let chill in the refrigerator until required.

• Unroll the sponge, then the mascarpone mixture over the sponge and sprinkle with the blueberries. Roll the sponge up again and transfer to a serving plate. Sprinkle with the almonds and dust with the confectioners' sugar. Decorate with the reserved blueberries and serve.

SERVES 6

9 oz/250 g fresh strawberries,
    plus extra to decorate
2 tbsp fruit liqueur, such as kirsch
    or crème de cassis

scant 2 cups heavy cream
4 squares bittersweet chocolate,
    melted and cooled
generous ½ cup raw brown sugar
fresh mint leaves, to decorate

Chocolate and Strawberry Brûlées

Freezing the brûlées before broiling ensures that the cream will not bubble up through the sugar. However, if you are short of time, it is not necessary to freeze them. You can caramelize the sugar using a culinary blowtorch.

• Pick over the strawberries and hull. Cut into halves or fourths, depending on their size, and divide between 6 ramekin dishes. Sprinkle over the fruit liqueur.

• Pour the cream into a bowl and whip until it is just holding its shape. Add the cooled chocolate and continue whipping until the cream is thick. Spread over the strawberries. Cover and freeze for 2 hours, or until the cream is frozen.

• Preheat the broiler to high. Sprinkle the sugar thickly over the cream, then cook under the broiler until the sugar has melted and caramelized.

• Let the brûlées stand for 30 minutes, or until the fruit and cream have thawed. Serve decorated with a few extra strawberries and some mint leaves.

SERVES 4

12 cape gooseberries

7 squares semisweet chocolate,
   broken into pieces

1 tbsp corn oil

12 small strawberries

Chocolate-Dipped Fruit

Large cherries would make a good alternative or addition to the strawberries and cape gooseberries.

• Line a baking sheet with nonstick parchment paper. Peel back the papery outer case from each cape gooseberry and twist at the top to make a "handle."

• Put the chocolate and oil in a small, heatproof bowl, then set the bowl over a pan of barely simmering water and heat until the chocolate has melted. Remove from the heat, then stir and let cool until tepid.

• Dip the fruit in the chocolate mixture and let any excess drain back into the pan. The fruit does not need to be completely coated.

• Set the fruit on the prepared baking sheet. If the chocolate forms a "foot" on the paper, it is too warm, so let cool slightly. If the chocolate in the bowl begins to set, warm it gently over the pan of simmering water. Chill the dipped fruit in the refrigerator for 30 minutes, or until the chocolate is set, then peel away from the paper. Serve on their own, or use to decorate another dessert.

SERVES 4–6

1 lb/450 g fresh blueberries, plus
    extra to decorate
²/₃ cup water
scant 1¼ cups superfine sugar
¾ cup crème de cassis
2 envelopes granulated gelatin
3 tbsp water

TO DECORATE

fresh mint leaves
confectioners' sugar, sifted,
    for dusting

Blueberry Jelly with Cassis

To make individual jellies, you can pour the fruit mixture into individual glasses or dishes and float the cream on top before serving.

• Put the blueberries, water, and sugar in a pan and cook over medium heat until softened.

• Remove from the heat and let cool. Crush the berries with a wooden spoon to make a smooth purée.

• Pour the purée into a measuring cup and add the cassis. Make the mixture up to 20 fl oz/600 ml, adding extra water if necessary.

• Put the gelatin and the water in a heatproof cup and soak for 1–2 minutes, or until it is spongy. Put the cup in a small pan with enough water to come halfway up the sides, and heat over low heat for 2–3 minutes, or until the gelatin has dissolved and the mixture is clear. Let cool until it is the same temperature as the fruit purée.

• Mix the blueberry mixture and the gelatin together and pour into a jelly mold or a glass serving bowl. Cover with plastic wrap and chill in the refrigerator until set. Decorate with fresh blueberries and mint leaves, then dust with sifted confectioners' sugar and serve.

SERVES 6–8
8 ladyfingers
generous ¼ cup raspberry jelly
⅔ cup crème de cassis or framboise
8 oz/225 g fresh raspberries
8 oz/225 g fresh strawberries

CUSTARD
generous 1¾ cups light cream
5 egg yolks
3 tbsp superfine sugar
½ tsp vanilla extract

TOPPING
1¼ cups heavy cream
2 tbsp milk
⅜ cup toasted flaked almonds

Berry Trifle

If you prefer, you can make the trifle in individual serving dishes instead.

• Break the ladyfingers into pieces and spread with the jelly. Put in a glass serving bowl and pour over the fruit liqueur. Pick over the berries and hull if necessary. Spoon on top of the sponge.

• To make the custard, heat the light cream in a small pan until just coming up to boiling point. Using a wooden spoon, beat the egg yolks, sugar, and vanilla extract together in a heatproof measuring cup. Pour the hot cream into the cup, stirring constantly, until well mixed. Return the mixture to the rinsed-out pan and heat very gently, stirring constantly, over the lowest heat until the sauce has thickened enough to coat the back of the wooden spoon. Put the bottom of the pan in a bowl of cold water immediately to prevent it overcooking. Stir until cooled.

• Pour the custard over the trifle base, then cover with plastic wrap and let settle in the refrigerator for 2–3 hours or overnight.

• Just before serving, whip the heavy cream with the milk in a bowl until thick but still soft. Spoon over the custard and swirl around using a knife to give an attractive appearance. Decorate with the toasted almonds, then cover with plastic wrap and chill in the refrigerator before serving.

SERVES 6
1 lb 9 oz/700 g fresh gooseberries
generous ½ cup superfine sugar
3 tbsp elderflower cordial
1¼ cups heavy cream

lemon balm or mint leaves,
    to decorate
crisp cookies or sponge fingers,
    to serve

Gooseberry Fool

Gooseberries are the traditional main ingredient in fruit fools, desserts made of cooked, puréed fruit folded into whipped cream, but you may try almost any mashed or puréed fruit.

• Trim the gooseberries and put in a pan with the sugar. Cook over low heat, stirring constantly, until the fruit is softened to a pulp.

• Remove from the heat and beat well with a wooden spoon until you have a thick purée. If you would like a smoother consistency, use the back of a wooden spoon to press the purée through a nylon strainer into a bowl to remove the seeds. Stir in the elderflower cordial. Taste for sweetness at this point and add a little more sugar if needed. Let cool.

• Whip the cream in a bowl until it is thick but not too dry. Using a metal spoon, gently fold in the cold gooseberry purée until only just combined—the fool looks more attractive if it has a marbled appearance.

• Spoon into 6 glass serving dishes or 1 large glass bowl, then cover with plastic wrap and chill well in the refrigerator. Decorate with lemon balm or mint leaves and serve with crisp cookies or sponge fingers.

SERVES 6

8 oz/225 g fresh red currants,
   plus extra to decorate

8 oz/225 g fresh raspberries,
   plus extra to decorate

¾ cup water

generous ½ cup sugar

⅔ cup cranberry juice

2 egg whites

fresh mint sprigs, to decorate

Red Berry Sherbet

It is possible to use a variety of soft fruit in this recipe, including black currants, strawberries, and blackberries, although you won't necessarily end up with a red berry sherbet!

• Strip the red currants from their stems using the prongs of a fork and put in a large, heavy-bottom pan with the raspberries. Add 2 tbsp of the water and cook over low heat for 10 minutes, or until softened. Using the back of a wooden spoon, press the fruit through a nylon strainer into a bowl to form a purée.

• Put the sugar and the remaining water in the rinsed-out pan and heat over low heat, stirring, until the sugar has dissolved. Bring to the boil, then boil, without stirring, for 10 minutes to form a syrup. Do not let it brown.

• Remove from the heat and let cool for at least an hour. When cold, stir the fruit purée and cranberry juice into the syrup.

• If using an ice cream machine, churn the mixture in the machine following the manufacturer's directions. When the mixture begins to freeze, whisk the egg whites until they just hold their shape but are not dry, then add to the mixture and continue churning. Alternatively, freeze the mixture in a rigid freezerproof container, uncovered, for 3–4 hours, or until mushy. Turn the mixture into a bowl and stir with a fork or beat in a blender or food processor to break down the ice crystals. Lightly whisk the egg whites until stiff but not dry, then fold them into the mixture. Return to the freezer and freeze for an additional 3–4 hours, or until firm or required. Cover the container with a lid for storing. Serve scattered with extra fruit and mint sprigs.

SERVES 6

generous ½ cup sugar

2½ cups water

1 lb 2 oz/500 g fresh gooseberries, not topped and tailed, plus extra to serve

½ cup elderflower cordial

1 tbsp lemon juice

few drops of green food coloring (optional)

½ cup heavy cream

ice cream cookies, to serve

Gooseberry and Elderflower Sherbet

When available, instead of the elderflower cordial, use two freshly picked and rinsed elderflower heads, tied together in a piece of cheesecloth, adding them to the pan with the gooseberries. Discard once the gooseberries are cooked.

• Put the sugar and water in a large, heavy-bottom pan and heat over low heat, stirring, until the sugar has dissolved. Bring to the boil, then add the gooseberries and simmer, stirring occasionally, for 10 minutes, or until very tender. Remove from the heat and cool for 5 minutes.

• Put the gooseberries in a blender or food processor and process until smooth. Using the back of a wooden spoon, press the purée through a nylon strainer into a bowl to remove the seeds. Let cool for at least an hour.

• Add the elderflower cordial and lemon juice to the gooseberry purée and stir until well mixed. Add the food coloring to tint the mixture pale green, if using. Stir the cream into the mixture.

• If using an ice cream machine, churn the mixture in the machine following the manufacturer's directions. Alternatively, freeze the mixture in a rigid freezerproof container, uncovered, for 3–4 hours, or until mushy. Turn the mixture into a bowl and stir with a fork or beat in a blender or food processor to break down the ice crystals. Return to the freezer and freeze for an additional 3–4 hours, or until firm or required. Serve with gooseberries and cookies.

SERVES 6

1 lb 9 oz/700 g summer berries, such
    as raspberries, blueberries,
    blackberries, and strawberries
generous ¾ cup superfine sugar
2 oz/55 g preserved ginger in syrup
ice cream cookies, to serve

VANILLA ICE CREAM

1 lb/450 g plain yogurt
scant 1¼ cups superfine sugar
1 vanilla bean
1¼ cups heavy cream

Hot Berry Compote with Vanilla Ice Cream

You could also use some red currants or black currants with the berries. The ice cream can be kept in the freezer for up to one month.

• Make the ice cream in advance. Pour the yogurt into a bowl and stir in ¼ cup of the sugar. Cut the vanilla bean in half lengthwise and scrape out all the seeds, then add them to the yogurt.

• Discard the bean. Whisk the cream in a separate bowl until thick but still soft, then fold into the yogurt mixture.

• If using an ice cream machine, churn the mixture in the machine following the manufacturer's directions. Alternatively, freeze the mixture in a rigid freezerproof container, covered, for 1 hour. Turn the mixture into a bowl and stir with a fork or beat in a blender or food processor to break down the ice crystals. Return to the freezer and freeze for an additional hour. Repeat until the mixture is completely frozen. Transfer the ice cream to the refrigerator 15 minutes before serving.

• Pick over the berries and hull if necessary. Put the fruit in a pan with the remaining sugar and heat over low heat until the sugar has dissolved and the fruit juices begin to run. Do not overcook. Finely chop the preserved ginger and add to the fruit. Put the ice cream in individual serving dishes, then pour over the hot compote and serve immediately with ice cream cookies.

Index